AMAZON INTERVIEW SECRETS

HOW TO RESPOND TO 101 POPULAR AMAZON LEADERSHIP PRINCIPLES INTERVIEW QUESTIONS

Martha Gage

CONTENTS

Introduction

There are over 20,000 job postings advertised on Amazon Jobs websites with a large variety and range of positions. However, as a trillion dollar company that is constantly ranked on top as one of the best places to work in the US, the competition to fill those positions in Amazon is equally high. Since the very inception of the company, Amazon has had a clear vision for its culture and exceptionally high standards for its employees, led by a comprehensive set of principles.

Following questions and answers are based fully on those Amazon Leadership Principles and inspired by real questions asked in Amazon interviews.

<u>Amazon Leadership Principles</u>

1. Customer Obsession
2. Ownership
3. Invent and Simplify
4. Are right, A Lot
5. Learn and Be Curious
6. Hire and Develop the Best
7. Insist on the Highest Standards
8. Think Big
9. Bias for Action
10. Frugality
11. Earn Trust
12. Dive Deep
13. Have Backbone, Disagree, and Commit
14. Deliver Results

101 Amazon Leadership Principles Interview Questions

1. Describe for me how you have demonstrated customer obsession?

Tip – As the very first Amazon Leadership Principle, Customer Obsession will surely be an on-going theme during your interview. Prepare with anecdotes that you can use to prove your customer-centric way of thinking.

Sample Answer – "In any given situation, I start with the customer and work backward. My sole intention is to provide an amazing customer experience, even if that means going out of my way to exceed their expectations on the service that I give them. I understand that it is not only about earning their trust, but also keeping their trust by consistently and continually providing great customer experience."

2. Walk us through a time when you helped a customer through a difficult process and what that looked like.

Tip – Pick a professional anecdote that shows a time you demonstrated both customer obsession and taking ownership of a situation. It should show your problem-solving skills and react quickly and successfully to a difficult situation.

Sample Answer – "A customer complained about a technical issue of a product and was clearly irritated since the product was brand new. It, however, turned out to be their lack of knowledge and practice in operating that product. I listened with understanding and took them through the process step by step with patience and care. I focused on making sure that the customer clearly understands and able to operate the product safely."

3.   **Tell the story of the last time you had to apologize to someone.**

Tip – This question focused on your ability to be vocally self-critical, which is an important leadership trait, especially when working with teams. Pick a situation where you did not only apologize but also took measures to successfully correct the mistake that happened.

Sample Answer – "I like sticking to tried and true methods when it comes to handling projects that I have previous experiences in doing. During a recent project, I rejected a different method of operation suggested by a new member thinking it would lower the quality of the final product even though it would have saved us a lot of time. However, during the last minute rush, we resorted to the new method, which ended up being a great success. I apologized to the new member on not having confidence in their method at first."

4. **When you are working with a large number of customers, it is tricky to deliver excellent service to them all. How do you go about prioritizing your customers' needs?**

Tip – Focusing on the leadership principles customer obsession, taking ownership, and innovation. Remember that you aim to be hired by the world's largest online retail company. Think big.

Sample Answer – "I believe in approaching each and every customer requirement with the same level of attention at first. Properly understanding the gap between importance and satisfaction is important when prioritizing each customer's need. I would give priority for the important and expected features or demands first, and fulfill the requirements focusing satisfaction and delight after. It is all about recognizing the vital few from the trivial many."

5. **Give me an example of a time when you did not meet a client's expectation. What happened, and how did you attempt to rectify the situation?**

Tip – Another question that requires you to be self-critical. When answering a question like this, be careful not to focus too much on the negativity. Elaborate on the positivity that

comes with identifying your mistake and taking
actions to make it right.

Sample Answer – "One time a client expressed that he is not fully satisfied with a web development project that my team and I delivered. We always made sure to involve the client in the design aspects from the beginning to the end. However, our User Interface designer had taken slight creative liberty when it comes to the layout to deliver a perfect outcome. I sat down with our designer and the client and explained the reasons for the few deviations of the design from what the client directly requested. In the end, the client decided not to change anything and admired the skills of the designer and thanked us for going an extra mile to make sure he gets a perfect outcome."

6.   **Tell me about a time when you changed your process to better align with customer needs.**

   Tip – This question also tackles your ability to take ownership of a situation and strategically make critical, and most importantly, customer-centric decisions.

Sample Answer – "A customer made an order related to their upcoming nuptials, and they needed it delivered on a particular date. While the delivery method that they selected did not offer close tracking to mention the exact date that they would receive the article, I put a little more effort and care during the logistics process to make sure that they receive the order on the day they specifically needed it. The client was extremely thankful."

7. **Tell me about a time you handled a difficult customer. What did you do? How did you manage the customer? What was her/his reaction? What was the outcome?**

Tip – Amazon is not a company that simply uses "customer-centric" as a tagline for marketing. When they say that they are customer obsessed, they truly mean it. It is extremely important to not put the customer in too much of a bad spotlight when you answer this question.

Sample Answer – "I once had a graphic design customer just seemed virtually impossible to impress. He paid great attention to detail and seemed to find problems in places that we never imagined. My solution was to get him fully on board in the process of design. We truly listened to his suggestions and made immediate changes when he requested. He ended up being great friends with our team in the end, and became a frequent repeat customer."

8. **Most of us, at one time, have felt frustrated or impatient when dealing with customers. Can you tell me about a time when you felt this way and how you dealt with it?**

Tip – This question covers your ability to be self-critical and your professionalism. Be honest. Amazon is a company that appreciates those who learn from their experiences and grows.

Sample Answer – "During my retail working days, I have had irritated customers with difficult expectations. During those times, I always remind myself that it is not a personal attack against me. I keep myself calm and collected, then try to be empathetic toward the customer. Being apologetic and actively sympathetic is important when handling such situations, and providing a solution as soon as possible."

9. **When do you think it is okay to push back or say no to an unreasonable customer request?**

Tip – Amazon is a company that is extremely customer-centric and looks for employees who are resourceful enough to deliver results even during the most difficult times. Therefore, saying no to a customer should always be a very last resort.

Sample Answer – "I, personally, believe that there is always a solution to a problem. Regardless of how difficult it is, I will truly try my best to fulfill a request by a customer or at least meet them halfway. I would say no to a customer only if their request is simply not realistic, or expected me to directly break company policies."

10. How do you develop client relationships?

Tip – This question covers the obvious customer obsession leadership principle as well as earning trust and delivering results.

Sample Answer – "I believe that when it comes to developing any kind of relationship, communication is the key. I will always be efficient with my communication in my client relationships with an attitude that shows them I truly value customer satisfaction. With my experience, I have learned that maintaining the integrity and being transparent with my objectives are also essential to developing good client relationships.

11. Tell me about a time you used customer feedback to change the way you worked.

Tip – When you answer interview questions, always show that you are confident about your expertise, and yet willing to learn and grow from your experiences. As a customer-centric company, the feedback from customers is extremely important at Amazon.

Sample Answer – "I tend to be a perfectionist in my work. The style of my work changed after a customer told me the details that I have to focus on vary from one customer to another and that I have to approach every project with a clear and open mind".

12. **Tell me about a time you had to compromise in order to satisfy a customer.**

Tip – Amazon explains in their leadership principles that they expect their employees to "work vigorously to earn and keep customer trust." This includes many practical compromises. Be honest with your answer.

Sample Answer – "When you work in retail, the amount of work almost triples during the holidays. As a manager, I tend to pride myself on providing a great work-life balance to my team. One time, however, I had to compromise the generous holiday vacation time for myself and the team to make sure one of my biggest customers meets their year-end goal. The large profit we made from that project made it all worth it."

13. **How do you get to an understanding of what the customer's needs are?**

Tip – As an Amazonian, you need to always listen to your customer and fully understand their needs. This includes understanding not only what they say, but most importantly what they do, not say.

Sample Answer – "As a web developer, I work with many clients without the technical knowledge of what they require and can only provide me with the details of the aesthetic that they expect in the final product. I believe that great customer service is not only about doing what they ask us to do but about anticipating what they truly require and exceeding their expectations."

14. How do you anticipate your customer's needs?

Tip – This question tap into both your customer obsession levels and also your innovation, thinking beyond the limits and delivering great results.

Sample Answer – "Knowing your customer is the key. I believe in getting to know my customer not only on a professional but also a personal level. It is important to understand their lifestyle and the way they think in order to truly anticipate their needs. I am always updated and on the lookout for the problems to solve and trends to follow in order to give exactly what the customer needs."

15. How do you honestly pursue customer feedback, not just solicit them for compliments?

Tip – The best customer feedback is not inherently positive feedback, but also neutral and honest feedback with constructive criticism.

Sample Answer – "I always start with making sure I provide a perfect service that encourages the customer to leave feedback on their own without having to solicit. When I do pursue feedback, I always do it with clear intent and a purpose, explaining to my customer that what I require is constructive feedback and not simply a positive comment."

16. How do you wow your customers?

Tip – This question gives you the opportunity to prove to the interviewer that you would go that extra mile in order to meet their most important leadership principle – customer obsession.

Sample Answer – "Giving the wow factor to a customer is all about pleasantly surprising them by providing a level of service that exceeds their expectations. This should be started with perfect delivery of service along with a positive addition that they do not usually get from the competitors. It could be anything from an incentive like a discount or an offer they were not expecting to a follow-up to ensure they are fully satisfied with the service."

17. **Tell me about a time a customer wanted one thing, but you felt they needed something else.**

Tip – While always giving the priority to understanding and delivering exactly what the customer asked and expected from you, make this an opportunity to show how your expertise on the task you are performing comes into play.

Sample Answer – "As a web developer, I have studied psychology and the behaviors of visitors who come to a website. When clients specifically ask me to use plenty of colors and graphics on their websites, I know by my experience that they will not positively affect their user interface. It is always less is more when it comes to UIs."

18. **When was a time you had to balance the needs of the customer with the needs of the business?**

Tip – This is a tricky question. At the end of the day, you are an employee of Amazon and you need to give priority to the best interests of the business. However, due to the customer-centric culture at Amazon, lean more toward benefiting the customer.

Sample Answer – "This is something that comes up mostly with product pricing and offering discounts and other incentives to the customer. My approach is always thinking about long-term benefits for the business and retention of the customer rather than making a short-term profit and losing the customer."

19. Give me an example of when you took a risk and it failed.

Tip – Be careful when you pick a situation here. Your aim should be to show that you are able to take the calculated risk even with the potential to fail and that you can be self-critical and turn a failure into a learning moment.

Sample Answer – "One time when the budget was tight I tried to lead my team to complete a task with fewer resources than it usually needs. What I believed was that if we work hard enough, we will be able to make up for the lack of resources. The project ended up being a failure. What I learned was to plan ahead for the budget and not be overconfident."

20. Describe a project or idea (not necessarily your own) that was implemented primarily because of your efforts. What was your role? What was the outcome?

Tip – Talk about a time that you took the lead and led a project into a success. Focus more on how your specific skills and efforts contributed to the success of that project or idea.

Sample Answer – "When I was in college, the students in my year started a monthly magazine to publish creative, social, and political expressions by the students. However, there was no theme or a focus for the project. I took the initiative to gather all the submissions under a theme and successfully publish the magazine, which is still active to this day."

21. Tell me about a time when you had to leave a task unfinished.

Tips – Frugality is one of the most important leadership principles at Amazon. It is not only about tangible resources, but also the time and the energy of the workers as well.

Sample Answer – "As an intern, I had to manually reorganize some of the written documents in a publishing company. Half way in I realized the important parts of those documents have already been digital preserved, which means my time could have been used more effectively. I informed my supervisor and then left the manual organization unfinished."

22. Tell me about a time when you had to work on a project with unclear responsibilities.

Tip – As a leader, there are tasks you have to undertake without any clear responsibilities which you have to take the ownership of.

Sample Answer – "In my first job, which was an entry-level position in a start-up company, I had a mix of seemingly unrelated tasks I had to complete every day. I eventually realized that they are usually done by a Public Relations professional. I took the initiative to fully perform my duties and I was soon promoted to be the Public Relations manager of the company."

23. **Give an example of when you saw a peer struggling and decided to step in and help. What was the situation and what actions did you take? What was the outcome?**

Tip – The tricky part of this question is making sure that you do not come off as a micro-manager, but as a helpful team worker who humbly offers help to strengthen a team.

Sample Answer – "While I can think of many situations I lend a helping hand, perhaps the most memorable would be helping one of the most experienced and senior members of my team to navigate through a new virtual management system. They were reluctant to ask for help, but was very thankful that I offered to take them through it until they fully got the hang of it."

24. Give me an example of a decision you owned, which had a long-term focus.

Tip – This question covers the leadership principles of insisting on higher standards, diving deep, and delivering results. Decisions that have long-term focus prove your dedication and loyalty for your workplace.

Sample Answer – "I was in charge of setting up the website for one of the companies I worked for. Without simply getting a basic website online, I took my time to properly optimize the website for search engines and include great quality content. While it took me more time and the budget was higher, that website still holds the highest rank in search engines due to me thinking long-term many years ago."

25. Provide an example of when you personally demonstrated ownership.

Tip – Ownership in the context of Amazon leadership principles is all about acting on behalf of the entire company. In a company with a scope as large as Amazon, they do not need employees that say, "that's not my job."

Sample Answer – "When I worked for an event management company, I made it my duty to always be proactive with networking with many individuals who attend events not because it was my job, but because the exposure was good for the company. I represented the company on many occasions and brought plenty of opportunities."

26. Tell me about a time you went above and beyond.

Tip – When you want to be a part of a company that is extremely selective with their employees, doing bare minimum does not suffice. You should be willing to go above and beyond in order to fully exceed the expectations of everybody to stand out from the rest.

Sample Answer – "I was working at a marketing company when the .com bubble occurred with extreme growth in the usage of the internet. I foresaw the potential and took the initiative to start a digital marketing department in the company, which grew to become the biggest revenue stream."

27. Tell me about a time when you took on something significant outside your area of responsibility. Why was it important? What was the outcome?

Tip – E-commerce is an ever-evolving industry that needs many new skills as it grows. Therefore, you need to prove that you have the capability to be resourceful and take up responsibilities outside of your expertise and comfort zone.

Sample Answer – "As a marketer with a degree in linguistics, one of the things that I always lacked knowledge of was programming. However, after I joined a tech startup, I did a great amount of self-learning, since I was in charge of the tech aspect of digital marketing as well. It greatly helped me further branch out my career path later on."

28. Tell me a time when you created an innovative product.

Tip – The definition of innovative and product are quite vague here, giving you the chance to be creative. What they are looking for is your ability to be creative and think outside the box.

Sample Answer – "When I worked for a startup incubator, we used to have plenty of brainstorming sessions for innovative ideas. A few of my ideas – including a community platform to get ongoing updates of local traffic and an easy way to top up mobile phones became quite successful once they were made into functional mobile applications."

29. Tell me about a time when you gave a simple solution to a complex problem.

Tip – This question is directly connected to the Amazon Leadership Principle, "Invent and Simplify." When you work for an innovative company like Amazon, you should always be externally aware and look for new ideas from everywhere that make your work more efficient and more effective.

Sample Answer – "One of the most recurring issues that I faced when working for a restaurant was conflicts with walk-in customers and overbooking issues online. Online bookings were handled off-site. As a solution, I suggested the online bookings be taken at the restaurant, where the booking executive can see the situation at the restaurant, which drastically reduced the conflicts."

30. Tell me about a time when you invented something.

Tip – You do not have to be too overwhelmed by this question. They, of course, do not expect you to invent something that changed the world! Simply tell about an original solution you brought to the table to resolve an issue.

Sample Answer – "While I'd love to have invented something as useful as the light bulb or the wheel, my innovations are far smaller yet they have helped me a lot to be more efficient. For an example, when I had to handle plenty of manual filing in a library, I invented a virtual system that helped me save a lot of time and resources in the long run."

31. Tell me about a time when you observed two business opportunities to improve ROI, and how did you determine they were connected.

Tip – This is about having a complete understanding of what brings revenue and also your observation skills to recognize opportunities and make connections.

Sample Answer – "When I worked for a web development company, I soon recognized that along with the development aspects of websites, there are also marketing and content aspects that we regularly outsourced. I pitched to the management that by offering those services in-house, there is a great potential to create two more revenue streams. It worked perfectly and made us into a one-stop shop for all the development and marketing needs, especially for startups."

32. Tell me about a time when you were wrong.

Tip – The interviewer expects to see how you can be honest and constructively self-critical here. Do not try to take a positive aspect and put it in a way that seems negative. Genuinely pick a time where you went wrong – most importantly, a time you accepted your mistake and grew from it.

Sample Answer – "One time I had to take the lead in a group project where we had to create a team presentation. I underestimated the time we should take for preparations, and ended up in a tight spot. I took the full responsibility for my mistake and did the best from the time we had and truly learned my lesson."

33. **Tell me about a time when you had to work with incomplete data of information.**

Tip – Amazon is a large data-driven company, and you are expected to work with a large amount of data every single day. This question examines your ability to innovate and be resourceful when you have incomplete data.

Sample Answer – "When I was working as a scheduler with over 50 weekly schedules belonging to employees of different departments, I had to work with plenty of incomplete data. I did a lot of guess work while closely observing and updating my notes, especially about the customer flow."

34. **How do you find the time to stay inspired, acquire new knowledge, and innovate in your work?**

Tip – Amazon looks for self-motivated employees who always find time and energy to learn and grow rather than staying in one position for years looking forward to retirement.

Sample Answer – "Over the years, I have learned to compartmentalize my brain in order to maintain clarity and work-life balance. I treat the time I get after work just as importantly, always finding time to elevate myself not only as a professional but also as a healthy human being with a thirst for learning. When you are enthusiastic about learning and manage your time well, there is enough and more time in the day to stay inspired."

35. Tell me about a time when you influenced a change by only asking questions.

Tip – As the saying goes, you never learn anything by simply talking, you learn things by asking questions. The answer to this question should show your curiosity to learn and your proactive approach to gaining new knowledge.

Sample Answer – "During my days as an intern in a large multinational company, I was with a team of fellow interns who were struggling, yet not daring enough to ask questions. By being the person who always asked questions on my own behalf and also of others, I managed to make plenty of positive changes in the way the company communicated with their employees."

36. **Tell me about a time when you solved a problem through just superior knowledge or observation.**

Tip – Pick a situation where your observation skills came in handy. It does not have to be a grand gesture. Even a simple situation, which worked well in your favor would do.

Sample Answer – "As a digital marketer, I have always prided myself on being very much up-to-date with the new knowledge that comes to the industry. I voluntarily seek knowledge and learn the new methods of marketing, which have always given my company a competitive advantage over other players in our industry."

37. **Tell me about a time when you had to deal with a poor performer on your team.**

Tip – The key here is to always recognize the strengths of the poorest performers. Amazon's culture usually gives employees an opportunity to prove their worth in different positions of the company if they show poor performance in one position.

Sample Answer – "There was once a very talented marketer who suddenly started performing increasingly poor. I knew that he had it in him, so I talked to him personally and got to know that he had a family member with a recently diagnosed terminal illness. I made sure the responsibilities he got were his strengths and gave him the time and the space he needed. He gained back his performance in due course."

38. Tell me about a time when you mentored someone.

Tip – Every great achiever is inspired by a great mentor. Amazon encourages and helps mentorships within the company.

Sample Answer – "I once mentored a promising young intern who was extremely proactive about his career growth. He was hired by his immediate manager after his internship and went on to get a few promotions within a span of two years while studying part-time to work on his master's degree."

39. Tell me about a time when you could have stopped working but persisted.

Tip – Amazonians are exceptional. They never do the bare minimum. They seek perfection, and once they achieve it, the push a little more to ensure they maintain that quality and bring even more value if possible.

Sample Answer – "After my first annual sales target was assigned to me in my very first job, I worked extremely hard and managed to reach the target number within a few months. I did not slow my efforts there and ended up tripling my target, which led me to a promotion."

40. **Tell me about a time when you couldn't meet your own expectations on a project.**

Tip – This question covers the Amazon leadership principles of insisting on a higher standard, thinking big, and taking ownership. Talk about a situation where you were self-driven with high standards for yourself.

Sample Answer – "I have always been my own toughest critic, and therefore, tend to have extremely high expectations for my performance. I remember a time in college where I set out to interview over 100 people for a questionnaire and failed to meet my target due to not having enough time. I still had one of the most diverse set of answers for the questionnaire, but I felt that I could have done more."

41. **Tell me about a time when a team member didn't meet your expectations on a project.**

Tip – Amazon expects each and every one of their employees to be leaders who direct themselves as well as their team toward success. A part of being a leader is having balanced expectations. Be honest about your experience here.

Sample Answer – "I used to face this mostly during my college years due to having teams with students that have drastically different motivation levels. I often had to complete a lot of work in group projects myself due to having over expectations about my team members. I have learned to always assign work that suits their own style and phase of work as a team leader now."

42. Tell me about a time when you proposed new business.

Tip – Amazon is one of the biggest entrepreneurship success stories in the world. They expect their employees to have a creative and extremely entrepreneurial mind in order to fully understand the culture within the company and to be self-motivated to take a business toward success.

Sample Answer – "After I completed my marketing degree, I had plenty of ideas to create a marketing company. As a way of differentiating the business from many other marketing firms, I proposed focusing solely on social media for startups, which is a smaller niche that we can laser focus on."

43. Tell me about your proudest professional achievement.

Tip – This is one of those times you can proudly exercise your bragging rights. Pick a time that you got rewarded for your expertise and hard work in your career.

Sample Answer – "I can name a few, but I believe my proudest professional achievement was getting the accolade of 50 best up and coming marketers in the country by a reputed institution, which led me to join a promising startup as a consultant and an equity holder."

44. Tell me about a time when you went way beyond the scope of the project and delivered.

Tip – More opportunity for you to show your interviewers how you stand out from the rest. Due to the many extremely skilled candidates you will be competing with, take advantage of questions like this to highlight your ability to go that extra mile, and follow the leadership principles of thinking big and delivering results.

Sample Answer – "Early in my career, I got the opportunity to handle all the public relation needs for an up and coming e-commerce brand. Their budget was not big, and I was asked to simply cover the basic social media posts until the budget became bigger. I used all my media contacts and affordable online tools to make their domain the highest in local search rankings. It is still high to this day due to my initial efforts."

45. **Describe how you would handle a busy situation where three people are waiting for help from you.**

Tip – Working for a company as big as Amazon requires a lot of multi-tasking. You should prove to the interviewer that you are able to properly prioritize and provide the same quality of service to customers regardless of how busy you are.

Sample Answer – "I will ask them to brief me about why they need me, and will prioritize them according to the urgency, importance, and how time-consuming the task is. I will try to give an immediate solution to defuse the urgency and also see the possibility to delegate the task, to get them all attended to at the same time without keeping the customer or the colleague waiting."

46. **Tell me about a time when you took a calculated risk.**

Tip – Calculated risk-taking is a big part of Amazon as a company since their inception also was a strategically taken risk. You should not show that you will put the company or your customers in danger by taking irresponsible risks, but that you have the ability to properly calculate the risk of a situation and attend to it accordingly.

Sample Answer – "In one of the big web development projects that I handled, I took a risk by introducing a completely novel user interface without any prior research or a trial. I knew that our client base is young and love daring changes, but there was always a risk. It got an absolutely positive reception from all our users, with a surge of new users as well."

47. **Tell me about a time you needed to get information from someone who was not very responsive. What did you do?**

Tip – Good communication skills are essential in every aspect of working at Amazon, let it be directly with your customers or working alongside a team.

Sample Answer – "I like to consider myself as a good communicator, who is persuasive and easy to approach. If a person on my team is not responsive, I will try to communicate with them in a way they prefer, rather than expecting them to communicate the way I am used to. It is all about interpersonal relationships and getting to know who you are working within a personal level."

48. **Tell me about a time where you thought of a clever new way to save money for the company.**

Tip – Frugality is an important leadership principle at Amazon. It is all about being resourceful and accomplishing more with less.

Sample Answer – "I used to work for a company that sent out press releases about new products and events quite often. We paid a monthly fee for a PR company that was a huge portion of our public relations budget in general. After I realized that what the PR Company accomplishes can be done with a few calls, I suggested hiring a paid intern for half the price they used to pay for the PR Company. It worked out really well."

49. **Tell me about a time when you had to work with limited time or resources.**

Tip – This is also an extension to check your way of approaching the frugality leadership principle. Pick a situation where you were resourceful and successful.

Sample Answer – "As someone who has worked in many startup environments, working with limited time, and resources have become second nature to me. I can particularly pinpoint a time I organized a large press conference and a product launch within a mere 4 days, which turned out to be extremely successful."

50. Tell me a time when you earned the trust of a group.

Tip – As the saying goes, talent wins games, but teamwork wins championships. As a leader, you need to earn the trust of a group in order to lead them well. Select a situation where you successfully gained their trust and led a group.

Sample Answer – "I remember the first time I was assigned to lead a team. I was the youngest person in the group and I could tell that many team members did not have confidence in me. I knew I had to earn their trust and went out of my way to make sure that the project proposal and the plan I created was exceptional. I worked harder than everybody and eventually gained the trust of all my team members, which led us to have the most successful project out of many."

51. What would you do if you found out that your closest friend at work was stealing?

Tip – A tricky question! The interviewer is trying to see how you approach loyalty – loyalty to your friend and loyalty to the company.

Sample Answer – "It will honestly be about the severity of the theft. If it is just a pen, I will lightheartedly let them know that it is not appropriate. If it is more severe, I will definitely report it to the authorities since I would be enabling a crime if I did not report."

52. **Tell me about a time when you had to tell someone a harsh truth.**

Tip – One of the most important duties of a leader is recognizing the strengths and weaknesses of their team, which often involves the need to have uncomfortable conversations. Express that you can handle such a situation professionally.

Sample Answer – "I once had to tell a particularly confident designer that his design projects needed more creativity and that he needed to refine his skills. I did that encouragingly with constructive criticism."

53. **Tell me about a time when you had to dive deep into the data and the results you achieved.**

Tip – Amazon is an extensively data-driven company. You should show that you not only know how to handle the data you are given but that you will go the extra mile to dive deep into it for the best results.

Sample Answer – "When I was on a game developer team, I took my time to personally meet the important demographics that came up as potential customers during surveys, and get personal comments on the beta product, and how they feel we can improve."

54. Give me an example of when you did more than what was required in any job experience.

Tip – This question taps into the leadership principle bias for action and diving deep. They require employees who push boundaries and go beyond their expertise, if and when needed.

Sample Answer – "As someone who has worked a lot in startup companies, I often have to go beyond my scope to make sure that things get done. I once used YouTube tutorials to put together an annual accounting spreadsheet when we did not have an accountant."

55. Tell me about the most difficult interaction you had at work.

Tip – In a company as large as Amazon, it is unavoidable to have daily interactions with many stakeholders. While being honest about the difficulty, make sure you showcase your ability to handle any interaction.

Sample Answer – "I once deescalated a situation involving a customer who screamed and was threatening to another employee by initially empathizing with her and offering a clear solution. She ended up apologizing to my colleague as well."

56. Tell me about a time when you did not accept the status quo.

Tip – From its very inception, Amazon was a company that challenged the status quo. They want their employees to think outside the box and bring innovation to the table.

Sample Answer – "One of the smallest and yet effective ways that I changed the status quo in a very hierarchy driven company I worked in was to invite the suggestions and ideas from even the most junior employees. We managed some big wins with their ideas."

57. Tell me about an unpopular decision of yours.

Tip – Amazon has always been known for encouraging its employees to be "peculiar." Therefore, do not be afraid, to be honest with your unpopular decision as long as it positively affected you or your employer.

Sample Answer – "As a graduate fresh out of college, I was not much aware of the "real" world. I made the unpopular decision to take a year off to travel the world, working along the way. That experience has been invaluable for all the later success in my life."

58. Tell me about a time when you had to step up and disagree with a team member's approach.

Tip – A leader should have the skill to not only work well alongside his team but also effectively disagree with them. After all, as long the Amazon leadership principles go, leaders, "are tight, a lot."

Sample Answer – "In a brainstorming session for a mobile app, a senior team member suggested an idea that would be offensive to a protected community. I showed him how the app will not do well among the socially-aware millennial crowd, which was the target market."

59. If your direct manager was instructing you to do something you disagreed with, how would you handle it?

Tip – Draw from a real-life situation to answer this question, but make sure to do it in a respectful and professional way, rather than opting for personal attacks.

Sample Answer – "I was handling an unsatisfied customer once, and disagreed with my manager on the way the situation should be handled. I did not question his authority in front of everyone. I took him aside and privately told him my opinion, which he agreed and went ahead with."

60. **Tell me about a time where you overcame an obstacle and delivered results.**

Tip – "Deliver Results" is one of the most important Amazon Leadership Principles. It does not matter how big or small the obstacle was, as long as you were smart and creative in the way you overcame it.

Sample Answer – "One time before the launch of an important project, pretty much everything that could go wrong, went wrong. I suggested everybody come up with alternatives for the obstacles. We managed to launch the project strongly and on time."

61. **What is the most difficult situation you have ever faced in your life? How did you handle it?**

Tip – Amazon's behavioral interview method is all about getting to know a person rather than simply judging them based on certifications and recommendations on paper. The interviewer expects you to be honest and professional in answering questions similar to this one.

Sample Answer – "I completed an internship in a foreign company. I barely spoke their language and had to face a complete culture shock as well. I faced it by fully committing to learning the language and improving my communication skills. I ended up getting a glowing recommendation in the end."

62. **Give me an example of a time when you were 75% of the way through a project, and you had to pivot strategy—how were you able to make that into a success story?**

Tip – Being resourceful, innovative and flexible are 3 of the most important qualities of an Amazonian. This question explores the leadership principles, "Invent and Simplify" along with, "Deliver Results."

Sample Answer – "I started a forum with a "sticky" model growth engine, which focused on retention rather than acquisition. However, the organic growth was too low than I initially expected. Then I used a few viral marketing methods, which ended up making the forum a great success."

63. **Tell me about a time you had to deal with a difficult customer.**

Tip – The very first Amazon Leadership Principle is, "Customer Obsession." Therefore, pick a situation where you made the customer satisfaction a priority no matter how difficult it was.

Sample Answer – "Once a customer yelled with anger due to not being able to return a product. I made sure I was calm and understood it was mere frustration on the customer's end. I listened to her concerns, and let her know that while I couldn't give a cash refund, she could still have store credit."

64. How do you resonate with the principle, 'Are right, a lot?'

Tip – This leadership principle is all about having strong judgment and good instincts about the work that you do, and the environment you work in. Do not be afraid to show your confidence in your expertise.

Sample Answer – "Due to my passion for learning and observation over the many years of my work, I believe that I have a great sense of instinct when it comes to my responsibilities. I continue to work on my expertise to maintain this confidence."

65. Which Amazon leadership principle do you resonate most with?

Tip – Every process and mechanism in Amazon, including simple everyday tasks are formed under the Amazon Leadership Principles. Show that you are not only aware of them, but also have an in-depth understanding of them.

Sample Answer – "While there are a few Leadership Principles I strongly resonate with, Delivering Results is the one that resonates the most. I have a deeply ingrained passion and drive to always deliver results, no matter how much effort that I have to put into it."

66. How did you solve a recent business problem?

Tip – Being up-to-date about your industry is important as an Amazon employee. Show that your problem-solving skills are current and that you can bring modern solutions to the table.

Sample Answer – "An automobile company had 80% of their marketing budget reserved for traditional methods when I joined. They were falling far behind the competition. I increased digital marketing up to 80%, and brought the highest revenue increase in the history of the company."

67. Tell me about a time when you showed customer obsession.

Tip – This is a straightforward question referring to the first Amazon Leadership Principle. Take advantage of it and give a well thought out answer.

Sample Answer – "When I was working at the software division of a bank, we had difficulty getting online customers due to the lack of user-friendliness of online services. I put the complete priority to surveys and developing an app and an online system that customers expected, rather than forcing one on them. It was immensely successful."

68. Tell me about a goal you had and how you achieved it.

Tip – From a company that started from a garage to what it is today, Amazon is all about having big goals and achieving them.

Sample Answer – "When I first started studying digital marketing 10 years ago, lots of people discouraged me. I was determined to make a career out of it and be an industry expert. I had a great level of knowledge by the time people realized the value of digital marketing, and I managed to become a consultant at a very young age."

69. Tell me about a time you worked on a team.

Tip – At Amazon, working on a team does not mean that your responsibilities get divided. It means that everybody puts 100% into the team.

Sample Answer – "One of the very first companies I worked for was a startup. It was only 4 of us working in a basement, working late into the night. There were times our ideas conflicted, but we ended up creating an app that we managed to sell for 6 figures."

70.   Share an example of how you were able to motivate an employee or a co-worker.

Tip – Amazonians guild, lift up, and lead each other. When you work in a team, sometimes you have to give the needed motivation to your co-workers, especially during difficult times.

Sample Answer – "One of my co-workers in a project struggled with confidence and taking criticism. Even the simplest criticism would demotivate him and reduce his quality of work. I showed him the strengths that he is overlooking in himself, which motivated him in both his professional and personal life."

71.   What was the last project you led and what was the outcome?

Tip – Be descriptive with your answer. Show that you are able to manage a team toward a goal and deliver positive results.

Sample Answer – "I was in charge of the annual client conference at my last job. Next year's sales largely depended on the success of the conference. While there were a few missed deadlines by my team members, we all managed to get together to deliver a conference that got plenty of positive reviews and raised good revenue."

72. **Describe a situation when you had to work effectively under pressure.**

Tip – In an ever-growing company like this, you will have to constantly work under pressure. When answering this question, relate it with Invent and Simplify Leadership Principle.

Sample Answer – "When I was working for an event management company, I had to take over an event where the performer had a conflict with the previous planner. The promotion had already been done and I had to fully organize everything from scratch on a tight deadline, which became a great success."

73. **How do you handle a challenge? Give me an example.**

Tip – This question requires you to show your problem-solving skills as well as critical thinking. In a fast paced company like Amazon, it is likely that you will have to face and handle challenges almost daily.

Sample Answer – "Once, a long-term client was going to leave us for a competitor. I personally took over that account and offered the best customer service, as well as a more refined payment plan I specially made for them. They stayed and doubled their business with us."

74.   Have you ever had to change the way you communicated with someone?

Tip – From Customer Obsessions to Earning Trust to Delivering Results, good communication is essential to surviving the Amazon culture.

Sample Answer – "As a millennial, I am used to communicating with instant methods, like text messages. I had communication issues with a senior team member since I was not getting the instant responses I expected with him. I changed into more verbal and one-on-on conversations, which drastically changed our work relationship."

75.   Tell me about a mistake you made. How did you handle the situation?

Tip – Focus more on the lessons you learned and the way improved yourself by what you learned through the mistake that you made. Be honest and take full responsibility.

Sample Answer – "During my very first internship, I completely underestimated the amount of preparation for presentations. I failed miserably the first one, and made up for it by fully preparing the next time. I received praise by my superiors."

76. What do you usually do when you disagree with someone at work?

Tip – In the Amazon culture, disagreements are not inherently bad. They hire decisive and confident employees who can disagree with their co-workers with logical reasons, and manage to communicate and work on those disagreements constructively.

Sample Answer – "My disagreements with co-workers are never personal, and I always communicate it to them clearly. I keep my professionalism at all times, and keep my mind open to hear their reasoning and come to a mutual agreement after a rational discussion."

77. Have you ever had to work with a difficult manager or co-worker? How did you respond?

Tip – A "difficult" co-worker is an extremely subjective opinion. Focus on how you managed to create a working relationship with them, rather than emphasizing on their difficulties. This answer should be more about you than them.

Sample Answer – "There have been times when my manager or co-worker's style of working did not match with mine. I always make sure I communicate well with them since most of those inconveniences are based on lack of communication or understanding."

78. **Tell me a challenge you had where the best way forward was not clear cut. How did you decide what to do?**

Tip – Amazon is an innovative company, which has pioneered many technological advances. Therefore, you will likely face many challenges that you need to make a path and lead, rather than following a clear path.

Sample Answer – "I once led a project that helped a fully traditional company to move their processes and marketing into the digital space. I created a successful strategy without a clear understanding of the customer response, which turned out to be successful in the end."

79. **Give me an example of something you tried to accomplish but failed.**

Tip – Every leader has had their fair share of failures over time. What made them successful was learning from those failures and rising above to be more organized and successful. Be honest, and focus on the things you learned.

Sample Answer – "When I was doing user surveys about a mobile app, I assumed that I would get clean data from them. This led us to make wrong predictions. What I learned was to never make that assumption again."

80. Give me an example of a time when you showed initiative.

Tip – Leaders take initiative. They do not wait around for others to take the lead while being passive bystanders.

Sample Answer – "As a college student, I had a difficult time deciding which career path I truly wanted to pursue. I took the initiative to meet up with mentors in each career field and asked if I can work-shadow them to get a clear understanding of their responsibilities. This immensely helped me in making my decision."

81. Give me an example of a time when you motivated others.

Tip – The interviewer wants to understand how you are able to motivate not only yourself but also your peers when working in a group or a team setting.

Sample Answer – "Once, when he had a very tight deadline and the team has already burnt out from hard work, I suggested we would have a big pizza party once we submitted the project. Simple incentive, but it did motivate everybody to go on full gear and get the project done ahead of the schedule!"

82. **Tell me about a time when you delegated a project effectively.**

Tip – As a company with a culture of community and teamwork, Amazon expects you to be able to effectively delegate tasks as a manager or a team leader without feeling the need to micromanage.

Sample Answer – "I started a magazine, which featured the best events in an event management company. The team I got was largely inexperienced for the task, but I recognized their individual skills and fully delegated the main tasks of the project. It became one of the most requested services for the company."

83. **Tell me about a time when you coached someone.**

Tip – Amazon is a company that has immense room to grow and go up the ladder for those who are passionate and skilled. Therefore, they expect employees to be able to quickly move up and coach others.

Sample Answer – "I was able to get a few quick promotions due to my expertise, and I was in the rare situation where I coached someone my own age. He had an insatiable drive to learn and grow, and quickly made his way to a managerial position under my guidance."

84. **When have you used your fact-finding skills to solve a problem?**

Tip – Due to the exponential growth of the internet, everybody has access to an unending pool of facts. However, show that you have the needed research skill to find the correct facts and data at the right time.

Sample Answer – One of the clients in my accounting firm was dissatisfied with the way we handled her tax returns, thinking we overlooked some essential data. I fully combed through her account to find all her data, and found out that it was her who failed to submit all the data to us."

85. **What is the worst mistake you ever made? What did you learn from it?**

Tip – One of the most important Amazon Leadership Principles is being vocally self-critical. Take the responsibility for your mistake and show that you have learned and grown.

Sample Answer – "I once lost the business of a huge potential client that we gave a presentation to. I took the responsibility for it and reached out to the client to see if there has been anything we could have done to change his decision, which happened to be the lack of examples we presented him. I used his feedback to change our strategies, and eventually land an equally big client later."

86. What one thing would you change about Amazon?

Tip – As a company that has continually worked toward innovation, Amazon welcomes constructive criticism. Be honest and rationalize your answer.

Sample Answer – "While I understand perfection is not possible to achieve, I will probably improve the product search feature on Amazon to be more user-friendly, customized, and simplified. I would like the option of seeing products that suit my personal preferences overseeing a sea of products that I have to choose from."

87. What experience do you have that would help you in this role?

Tip – Use your familiarity with the Amazon Leadership Principles here. Show how you have practiced that principle in your previous positions, and how you can bring that experience to the table.

Sample Answer – "I have worked in retail for many years, and providing 1005 customer satisfaction is a task that I am very well trained in. I can bring my real life experience to this virtual platform which will multiply that."

88. **What was your worst group experience? What have you learned from it?**

Tip – Pick a real-life scenario, and focus mostly on the lessons that you learned.

Sample Answer – "When I was in college, I had a group presentation to be done with a set of fellow students. It was the first semester of the freshman year and I did know them personally. I delegated the tasks, and on the day of the presentation nobody had anything prepared but myself. I learned to never assume another person's dedication to work."

89. **Give an example of a time when you had too many things to do and you were required to prioritize your tasks.**

Tip – One of the most important qualities when it comes to time management is the ability to prioritize. You have to be pragmatic with your prioritizing when it comes to working in a fast-paced company like Amazon.

Sample Answer – "In an extremely demanding job position that I worked in where I had to multi-task at all times, I used to sit down for a few minutes every morning with my boss and get his input on what my priorities should be."

90.   How do you resonate with the principle "Invent and Simplify?"

Tip – The more you can show familiarity with Leadership Principles, the better. Try any anecdotes you have and show that you have done your homework.

Sample Answer – "Invent and Simplify" is a Leadership Principle I have practiced since I was young. My mind is wired in a way that it sees the most convenient way to do something at all times. I love being on the lookout for innovative ways that make my job easier and better in quality."

91.   Are you willing to work on your feet for ten hours, four days a week?

Tip – This is somewhat of a tricky question. It asks not that you will or you can, but if you are willing to. Give a logical answer rather than simply agreeing with everything just so you can get the job.

Sample Answer – "I certainly have the ability to do that if my job demands it. In fact, I often find myself more productive on my feet. So, yes, I am willing to and able to, but I hope it will not come to that."

92.   How do you persuade people?

Tip – Use examples to show the times you successfully influenced people in a positive way.

Being data-driven is better than being opinion-driven when you answer this question.

Sample Answer – "I faced difficulties accessing internal data in a different department when I was an intern. I made an appointment with the department head and put forth my reason to acquire data in a clear, concise, and logical way, which persuaded her that I do know what I am doing."

93. Tell the story of the last time you had to apologize to someone.

Tip – Show your ability to be vocally self-critical. A true leader not only learns from their mistakes but also build and maintain the relationships they make along the way by apologizing for mistakes and appreciating good work.

Sample Answer – "Paying recognition to the right people for the right thing is something that is very important to me. Once as a manager I praised someone for something they falsely took credit for. I sincerely apologized to the person who actually did the job."

94. What is the most difficult situation you have ever faced in your life? How did you handle it?

Tip – Do not go on the emotional road when you answer this question. Rather, use a professional anecdote and focus on the way how it helped you change and be a better person.

Sample Answer – "When I was working in a startup company that I helped launch, we faced losing the entire property over a fire. It was one of the most difficult times due to us putting so much work into that company. We managed to rise from the ashes and go on to become even more successful after."

95. Amazon is a peculiar company. What is peculiar about you?

Tip – By "peculiar" they mean that they think outside the box, and strive for action in a way that "normal" people do not.

Sample Answer – "In a culture of expecting a lot while doing the bare minimum, I am someone who finds joy in working hard. I am known for looking forward to Mondays, which is considered to be extremely peculiar by many."

96. What metrics do you use to drive change?

Tip – Amazon is a very much data-driven company. It is not enough to have the passion to drive change, but you should have a plan and a strategy to do so.

Sample Answer – "As a software developer, I generally use the metrics deployment frequency, the time it takes to experience full recovery, and also cultural metrics to fully drive change in my team."

97. Tell me about a project that went beyond your scope of work.

Tip – There are thousands of candidates who interview to get a position at Amazon. Therefore, recruiters look for those who go above and beyond the scope for the work that they do.

Sample Answer – "As one of the junior staff members in a restaurant, I had to take feedback from at least 10 customers a day about a change to restaurant layout. I went on to taking feedback from every single customer who came to the restaurant, staying past my allocated time as well."

98. Tell me about a time you had to deal with ambiguity.

Tip – While being data-driven is one of the key aspects of Amazon, there are times that you might have to work with ambiguity, especially when it comes to venturing into new and innovative technologies.

Sample Answer – "Once we had to isolate one customer segment in a marketing campaign due to a budget restriction, without enough data to determine which level would work the best. I used all the existing data to make an educated guess, which worked out successfully in the end."

99. Describe a situation where you had to make a decision without data.

Tip – Working with existing data is an important skill, and it is even more valuable to have the skill to work effectively even when there is not enough data.

Sample Answer – "There was one component missing from a grant application that I had to submit while my boss was away and not reachable. I used all the previous applications to fill out the component, and submitted the grant on time, which we ended up getting."

100. How do you motivate people?

Tip – As a company, Amazon inspires and motivates people every single day to be better. The company expects the same from its employees as well.

Sample Answer – "I like motivating people by being an example. I never preach about working hard and being successful, but I actually go out there and hustle every single day towards my goals, which has motivated many people according to what they have personally told me."

101. Tell me about a time you solved a complex situation with a simple solution.

Tip – "Invent and Simplify." At Amazon, you are expected to be on the lookout for simple solutions for even the most complex of problems, just like Amazon's entire platform that makes people's lives easier every single day.

Sample Answer – "My company faced an issue of low customer retention. When I individually inquired every single client about their reason to leave, it was about not building personal trust with the company. I called every account manager to send personalized reports to clients bi-weekly, which gave a huge boost of customer retention within a year."

Conclusion

Amazon recruitment process is largely based on behavioral based interviewing. It simply means that they consider the past behavior of a person to be the best predictor of their future behavior.

Amazon Leadership Principles are the strong foundation upon which this massive company is built. They are used daily in the decision-making process of the company, and all the candidates for Amazon job positions are evaluated based on them. Therefore, get extremely familiar with Amazon Leadership Principles, and make sure you have a good amount of anecdotes from your previous work experiences that support the principles.

Good luck!

Made in the USA
Las Vegas, NV
06 May 2022

48528898R00038